GIRL

GIRL

by
Wendy Jett

Accents Publishing • Lexington, Kentucky • 2022

Copyright © 2022 by Wendy Jett
All rights reserved

Printed in the United States of America

Accents Publishing
Editor: Katerina Stoykova-Klemer
Cover Art: Stevie Sidney

Library of Congress Control Number: 2022948003
ISBN: 978-1-936628-96-4
First Edition

Accents Publishing is an independent press for brilliant voices. For a catalog of current and upcoming titles, please visit us on the Web at

www.accents-publishing.com

Contents

Pray / 1
>Little Boy Blue
>Misfortune

Reborn / 6
>Grace Is Amazin
>Mama's Magnificent Macaroni & Cheese

Revelation / 11
>Our Father
>Doctrine

Dragonflies / 16
>Dragonfly Lullaby
>Miscalculation

BillyWade / 21
>Granny Faye's Perfect Pie
>Little Jack Horner

Petey / 26
>Sanctuary
>Genesis

The Visit / 32
>State Fair Apple
>ReVisited

Daddy / 37

> Night
> Daddy's Day After Drinkin Breakfast

Talkin / 42

> Listenin
> Daughter

Daisy / 48

> Jump Rope
> If You're Mad at Your Daddy Clap Your Hands

Mama Says / 53

> Boy
> Girl

Fate / 59

> Dragonfly Lullaby Reprise
> Little Boy Blue Reprise

Faith / 64

Acknowledgments / 68

About the Author / 69

Pray

• *Wendy Jett*

The only time an elephant was in this county was the year I was born. Well, that's what Mama says. She says she was as big as an elephant when she was carryin me. Ankles all swole up, face fat as a well-fed hog. Biggest pregnant woman this side of the Missisippi. Granny Faye called her "Big Mama" til the day I was born.

I came burstin outta her body, screamin like a skinned rabbit. Mama says that was the best day of her life. All she ever wanted was a baby girl. She got what she wanted. Me.

Course Daddy wanted a boy. Somebody to shoot with. Somebody to help work on the truck. Somebody to set fence posts. I've told Daddy hundreds of times, I can shoot. I can work on the truck. I can dig post holes. Daddy just says, "Git girl. Go find your mama."

Mama's tried to birth a boy. Twice. But they was born without a soul. Never took one breath in this world. Just stayed right there in heaven. Watching Mama cry and Daddy slam doors. Them baby boy bodies are layin in the ground just past the big Oak. Sleepin for eternity.

Sometimes I see Daddy talkin to them boys. I'm not sure what he's sayin, but I see his lips movin. Daddy bows his head, like he's prayin, but Daddy never prays. He says there's nothin to pray to. He says there ain't no God. Daddy says, if there was, he'd have a son.

But I know there's a God. I'm sure of it. The only thing powerful enough to make the trees, the mountains, the frogs at the creek and the night sky, is God. There ain't no other explanation. There's too many wonderous things in the world for it to just be an accident. It has to be the power of God. You can feel the power of God in the wind. Smell the power of God in a rose. Taste the power of God in one of them fresh peaches. Oh, I'm sure there's a God. I'm sure that God listens to my prayers. He's waitin for the perfect time to say, "Ok, girl, here you go. I heard you."

I pray for Mama to grow a boy baby in her body. I pray for a soul to jump right outta heaven into that boy body. I pray that the baby boy screams like a skinned rabbit when he's born. I pray for that baby boy to take a big gulp of air on this earth. I pray for that baby boy to grow every day. Eat, and sleep, and play. I pray for that baby boy to be able to shoot. To be able to work on the truck. To be strong enough to dig fence posts. I pray for my daddy to get his baby boy. I know God's listenin. I know he will give Daddy his boy when it's time. I just hope it's soon, for Daddy's sake.

• *Wendy Jett*

Little Boy Blue

Come meet your daddy
Little Boy Blue
My heart is achin
I been waitin for you

Long fishin poles
And an old baseball glove
Are here for the boy
That I'm ready to love

Jump from the heavens
Take the leap son
I'll be here to catch you
Oh my beloved one

Misfortune

Yes, it is
an unfortunate event
when the brother
you never knew
dies before you
were born
and the son
your father always wanted
is replaced
by a daughter
he isn't sure what to do with.

Reborn

I tried to scream for Mama, but the water was in my throat. It was in my nose. It was in my ears. His hand was holdin me under. I could hear someone yellin, but I didn't know what they was sayin. I tried to be brave. I tried to be courageous. But I couldn't breathe. So I just started kickin. Bout that time, my body was pulled straight up outta that water to the thunderous sound of my Granny Faye yellin "Praise Jesus, praise Jesus. A soul is reborn!" I didn't know being reborn was so hard.

Pastor John patted me on the head and said, "Go with God, Girl." I could feel the mud squish between my toes as I made my way back up to the bank. Mama hugged me and wrapped me in a blanket. Spring baptisms are always cold. The water still carries the snowflakes and ice from winter. Sometimes you can still see your breath at a spring baptism.

Best thing about baptisms is the food. Being reborn makes a body hungry. God feeds the soul, but family feeds the body. Mama let me pick my baptism food. Macaroni and cheese. Ain't nothin better than Mama's macaroni and cheese. Course we only taste that at Christmas, but today is special. I have been reborn. My body needs that macaroni and cheese. So creamy and thick you can stand on it. A crunchy layer of cheese on the top so you have to cut it with a knife to start. Big noodles that look just like the pipe under the kitchen sink. Melted cheese all shoved down in them pipes. Just oozin with deliciousness. One bowl will not fill this reborn body.

Daddy loves macaroni and cheese, but he don't like baptisms. Says baptisms are for the weak who need something to cling to. Says those folks are just like the kudzu that chokes a tree. Twistin itself all around the tree to survive, until it just plum kills the tree. Then it moves on to another tree and does the same thing. Daddy says church folk can just twist the life out of you if you let em. I might be reborn, but I ain't gonna twist the life outta nobody round here. I like church folk. They carry God in their heart, even if they do get a little loud sometimes.

Last Sunday, Roberta Johnson started speakin in the Holy Language. She was so loud that Pastor John had to slap her back to earth. She was floatin out in the heavens. Talkin to God and the angels. Speakin words I never heard. Rollin round on the floor. She was so filled with the Holy Spirit, I was scared God himself might just burst through the door and take her home. Sister Johnson said she don't remember even one minute of it. Said if it weren't for the mark on her face, she wouldn't believe a word of it.

Now that I'm reborn, I sure hope I don't start speakin in the Holy Language. Daddy won't have none of that in his house. I pray the Lord keeps my reborn soul safe in his arms and my tongue quiet in Daddy's house.

Grace Is Amazin

Amazin Grace,
how sweet the sound
Of the wind in the
leaves on the trees.

Amazin Grace,
your arms wrapped around
A poor, wretched girl
soul like me.

Grace is amazin,
take me home
To the land where
worries are relieved.

Amazin Grace,
I am now born again
Of this I am sure and
I believe.

• *Wendy Jett*

Mama's Magnificent Macaroni & Cheese

1½ cups cooked macaroni
the kind that looks like a pipe under the sink

2 cups milk
¾ lb of Real New York Sharp Cheddar Cheese
4 pinches of salt
2 big tablespoons of butter
4 tablespoons flour

Cook the macaroni pipes and pour out water
Put in a oven dish

Warm the milk on low flame while you cut
up the cheese in little bits
Put the cheese in the milk and stir it
Mix the flour with a little water to make a paste
and put in the milk
Stir and stir til smooth then pour over the macaroni
Cover it with more cheese bits, cover it real good
If you want to, you can put some stale bread crumbs on
the top

Bake 350 degrees for 20-25 minutes

Revelation

• *Wendy Jett*

Daddy had a fistful of her hair and was pullin her to the truck. Mama didn't say a word. I was runnin fast as I could to keep up. Daddy'd just leave me behind if I didn't get to the truck in time. I knew better than to get up front, so I just sat in the bed.

I could hear Daddy growlin at Mama. He said he saw her makin eyes at Jimmy Lainhart. He said that no man needs five handmade baskets. That Jimmy was just buyin them cause he had heat for her. Mama said he bought them baskets for his mama and granny. Daddy just slapped her right cross the cheek. Mama didn't say another word all the drive home.

I can't stop thinkin bout it. It don't matter that I'm tucked in bed. It don't matter that the house is quiet. I just can't stop thinkin bout it. Mama don't have eyes for Jimmy Lainhart. She loves Daddy, even with his mean streak. She's a strong and righteous woman. Everybody loves Mama. She can't help it. Granny Faye says God added 2 scoops of kindness when he made Mama.

Mama's famous in these parts. Her baskets are as pretty as an April flower. She says she weaves love in them baskets. I believe it! People drive two counties to buy one of Mama's baskets. They can only buy them at the Church's fundraiser every year, so they make sure they get there early. Mama always sells them all. Daddy don't seem to mind the money she gives him. So why should he mind who she sells them to? I think Daddy's lettin Satan sit on his shoulder and whisper in his ear. Sometimes you just hafta knock Satan off and let them angels take his place.

I'm gonna get myself up fore sunrise and make Mama some breakfast. She loves eggs and biscuits. Blackberry jam is her favorite. Mine too. Mama says we were cut from the same cloth. I sure hope she's right. I want to grow up to be a strong, smart woman like her. I don't want my daddy's mean streak, but sometimes I feel it growin down in my bones. Specially when I hear him growlin at Mama, I can feel myself burnin.

I best say my prayers two times tonight. God needs to know I'm serious bout it. Guess I need to say a special prayer for Daddy. Mama would want me to.

• *Wendy Jett*

Our Father

who art in heaven/watch
over my mama/take
those mean bones out of
my daddy/bury
them in the dirt/cover
them up real good so he can't
get em/help Mama's kind
heart stay pure/make me more
like my mama/please give
my daddy patience/help him repent
for his bad ways/keep us
safe and fed/thank you for
the trees and creek and hills/watch over
my Granny Faye and Grandpap/praise
be to God and his angels/thank you Lord
for listenin to my prayers/help me
be righteous and humble/I pray
in your name/A
men/goodnight/

Amen

Doctrine

He sees
a thorn bush
with
a rose.

She sees
a rose bush
with
a thorn.

Dragonflies

Girl •

Dragonflies are sacred. Like the Holy Spirit. Granny Faye says they carry angels from heaven to check on us. She says them angels whisper in our ear while we're sleepin. They tell us stories bout heaven and give us messages from people that passed. Granny says, "take notice of a dragonfly, girl. Don't swat at em. Listen to em."

Last time I saw a dragonfly, it told me Mama was gonna birth a baby. Baby Petey came in this world screamin and a kickin with a little dragonfly mark of birth on his forehead. Mama said, that mark shows that he was a gift from the angels. I think she's right. Petey is God's gift to Daddy.

Granny Faye said her daddy had a dragonfly mark of birth on his head too. Her daddy passed a long time ago, fore I was born. He drown in the river tryin to save a calf. Calf drown too. They went to heaven together. Granny thinks Petey musta known her daddy in heaven. I'm not too sure bout that.

I get to keep watch on Petey while Mama cleans the clothes. He's a good baby. Don't cry much. He loves to sit on the porch with me and count the swallas in the yard. Sometimes I run my finger over that dragonfly on his head while I pray. I pray for God to keep Petey safe. Daddy can't take losin another boy baby.

I wish I had a dragonfly mark of birth on my body. I wish I was sent from the angels, like Petey. He's special. I ain't special. I'm like everybody else. Just a girl that grew in her mama's belly from the seed of the forbidden apple. The apple from the Garden of Eden. All mamas have them seeds in their bodies. When mamas are taken over by earthly temptations, them seeds sprout and grow a baby. Earthly temptations can destroy us if we're not careful. Pastor John says we must be strong against earthly temptations. Temptations like drinkin whiskey and takin the Lord's name in vain. Temptations like stealin from your neighbor or not listenin to your daddy. We must be strong and walk with God.

I ain't seen a dragonfly in a long time. Granny Faye says they must be visitin somebody else right now. She says, "Be patient girl. Walk with God. He will send you a message soon, on the wings of a dragonfly."

Dragonfly Lullaby

Sweet lil baby, don't you cry,
You got the mark of the dragonfly.

Brought from the heavens, on a prayer,
Proof is in the mark of birth you wear.

Dragonfly, dragonfly, Angels sing,
Angels a sittin on a dragonfly wing.
Dragonfly, dragonfly, Angels sing,
Angels a sittin on a dragonfly wing.

Sweet lil baby, here in my arms,
I won't let you come to any harm.

Oh, Mama and Daddy love you boy,
You are a dragonfly that brings us joy.

Dragonfly, dragonfly, Angels sing,
Angels a sittin on a dragonfly wing.
Dragonfly, dragonfly, Angels sing,
Angels a sittin on a dragonfly wing.

• *Wendy Jett*

Miscalculation

A lone
dragonfly

skates across
the murky, stagnant
water of the lopsided
birdbath, oblivious
to the fact
that it is now lunchtime.

BillyWade

• *Wendy Jett*

Four eyes. Big head. Thick. Slow. Doofus. Stoopy. Retard. Jackass. BillyWade's been called every one of them names at school. Ms. Schafer don't do nothin to them boys that tease him. She just tells BillyWade to toughen up and close his ears.

There's been many a times them boys chased both of us all the way up the road to Granny Faye's place after school. Throwin dirt and rocks at us, and spittin on us if they get close enough. Granny Faye says to pay them no mind. She usually follows that up with a slice of pie. BillyWade says all that teasin is worth it just to get that first warm bite.

Granny Faye says God touched BillyWade when he was born, so he's different. She says BillyWade still has one foot in heaven, so he don't understand everythin here on this earthly plain. She says I won't never find a truer friend than BillyWade. I think she's right.

Last spring BillyWade was the one that pulled me outta the sink hole. We went down there to toss in Daddy's old tire. But that hole bout swallowed both us. BillyWade grabbed hold of the tree root and fought like a bear. He let me climb right over him onto the ground. Then we pulled and tugged til he was able to get out. Sat right there on that bank together. Laughed til we cried. Made the blood bond swear to never tell no one what happened. Specially my daddy.

Girl •

My daddy's got no patience for BillyWade. Says he shoulda been born a girl cause he can't do the things boys should do. BillyWade can't work on a truck or fix a tractor. He just don't have the brain for it. But BillyWade sure can paint pictures. Pictures of God's glorious world. Big fields of corn blowin in the wind. Angry Blue Jays chasin the Robins. The water leapin off the rocks as it rushes down the hill. That boy's got a gift for paintin.

BillyWade says he's filled with the Holy Spirit when he paints. Sometimes he has to get up in the middle of the night and sneak into his closet to paint. Says God just keeps callin his name til he does it. I've watched BillyWade paint with his eyes closed. No peekin at all! He says the Holy Spirit just moves his hands for him. He says if he lost his hands, he would paint with his feet. He says paintin "restoreth his soul."

His daddy left when BillyWade was 2 years old. Left his mama with BillyWade and a stack of bills. Well, that's what Granny Faye says. She says BillyWade's daddy fell in love with a man that worked on the railroad. He hopped a train and went off to make a new life. Granny Faye says, "We don't pass judgement on people. We leave that to God. We just love and care for those in our lives." I think Granny Faye might be the smartest woman in this county. I'm gonna ask BillyWade to paint a picture of my Granny. She's special, and so is he.

• *Wendy Jett*

Granny Faye's Perfect Pie

4 cups of peeled, diced apples from Grandpap's trees
2 cups of peeled, diced sweet potatoes from Granny's garden
½ cup sugar
¼ cup brown sugar
2 TB flour
1 TB lemon juice from a soft lemon
¾ t cinnamon and a pinch more
¼ t nutmeg
2 pinches of salt

Mix and pour into Granny's pie crust. Cover with another pie crust and brush some melted butter across the top. Cut out windas in the crust for the steam. Sprinkle a touch of brown sugar on the top crust.

Bake at 425 degrees for 45 minutes at Granny's house, 40 minutes at Mama's house cause her oven's too hot.

(Pie is better with Grandpap's homemade vanilla ice cream on top, but don't tell Granny.)

Little Jack Horner

Little Jack Horner
Sits in the corner
Playing there all alone
Cause he's on the spectrum
He gets no direction
We simply toss him a bone

Petey

Girl •

It's been 4 hours, 23 minutes and 32, 33, 34 seconds since I seen Petey. Me an Mama have looked all over for him. The barn, the shed, the doghouse, behind the pine tree at the edge of the drive. He ain't in any of them regular places. We been callin and callin for him. No answer. Petey always answers Mama.

Course Daddy is beside himself. Says he ain't losin one more boy to a selfish God. He even got his gun outta the house. Now he and Grandpap and Daisy are searchin the woods toward the creek. Me and Mama are going toward the butterfly field. Granny Faye and BillyWade are stayin on the porch in case Petey shows up. He has to be gettin hungry.

I can hear Daisy a barkin and Daddy hollerin, so they ain't gone too far. I been prayin as fast as I can. Mama says we just have to put our faith in God that he will hold Petey in his arms and keep him safe. Petey's never wandered off before. Never.

I've always wandered off. Mama says I'm lookin for somethin in my life. I'm not sure what she means by that. I've got a good life. Can't imagine what I'm missin. Course lots of people spend their lives wanderin. But most of em's lookin for God. That's what Pastor John says anyway. There was people in the Bible that wandered for 40 years in the desert lookin for God. They just walked round and round in circles tryin to figure things out. All the time they just needed to open their hearts to find God. It ain't that hard to find God. You just hafta look around you. The sky. The wind. The water. The desert sand. God holds space in all them places. Course if you keep your heart closed, Satan seeps in through them little cracks and builds a fortress. Satan is strong. The best way to defeat Satan is to not let him in in the first place. Keep God in your heart and Satan a stone's throw away.

The butterfly field is just ahead. Petey loves that spot. A rainbow of colors shoot up outta that field every spring. Butterflies of all shapes and sizes and colors come together, take flight and dance through that field.

I don't see Petey nowhere, but it looks like somethin's been through here. The grass is all pushed down.

"Petey, baby! Petey!" Mama is startin to sound scared. "Petey, answer me honey!"

I make my way to the edge of the field just where the trees start linin back up. Then I hear it. Barely.

"Mama. Mama." A tiny voice comin from the edge of the trees. Petey.

There he is sittin on the ground. Legs crossed. Somethin on his lap.

"Mama! He's over here!" I wave for Mama to come to me. She starts a runnin.

It's a fawn. A newborn fawn, layin on Petey's lap. "She's hurt, Mama." Petey points to the fawn's leg. All twisted and mangled. Musta run into a wild dog or a trap somewhere. "I didn't wanna leave her." Petey runs his hand across the deer's head and down her back.

"Baby, I'm just glad we found you! It's ok. We'll take care of both you. Girl, run down to the creek and tell your daddy we found Petey. I'll take the deer back to the house. Let's go boy." Mama bends over to pick up the fawn and just stops.

"Well, I'll be." Mama points to the fawn's back. There it is. Sittin dead center in the middle of her creamy, brown back. A white spot. A mark of birth. A dragonfly.

- *Wendy Jett*

Sanctuary

I stumble and cry
within the cobbled and crooked
path. Search for the compass
sun to guide my weary legs. Fall.
Creep on scarred knees for so long
I forget how to stand. Tip
my head back. Hiss at the moon

through salty eyes. Breathe in.
Breathe out. Pray for
forgiveness. Pray
to forgive. Ascend mountains.
Traverse rivers. Pull thistles from
my heart. Burrs from my
hair. I am searching for

my purpose. My journey
has only begun.

Genesis

And God said
I will break fragments
from my rainbows. Bless
them with wings
and a gentle spirit. They will

sip golden nectar from
glorious flowers. Pollenate
my gardens with
delicate feet.

       Flit
              Float

through the spring breeze
summer sun. As their
life cycle concludes they will
become nourishment for
my other creations.

I will call this
magnificent design

       The Butterfly.

The Visit

Girl •

I am flyin. Arms stretched wide. My belly skippin cross the tree tops like a flat rock bouncin over the water. The sun warm and high in the sky. I didn't know flyin would be so easy. This must be why birds sing. The joy of flight just fills your soul so full that you have to sing!

I can see Granny Faye's place ahead. The barn with rows of sunflowers just outside the door. Liftin their faces to the clouds. The well where, even in the dead of summer, the water is so cold it makes you shiver. I can see Midnight gallopin through the south field. Kickin her heels up, dancin in the wonder of the day. This must be what heaven feels like. Flyin through God's beauty. God's glory creepin into every part of your soul.

There's Grandpap. Head tucked under the hood of the truck. Grandpap says he's spent more time under the hood of the truck than he ever spent under Granny Faye. I'm not sure just what that means, but it always makes Granny Faye laugh. She says, Grandpap has calloused hands, but a soft heart.

I think that's Buckeye. Sleepin on the side porch. Tail waggin. He must be dreamin of them rabbits he chased last Sunday. Nearly caught one. Grandpap says that dog ain't no huntin dog. Says Buckeye would rather have the rabbit as a friend, than for his dinner.

The creek sure is pretty from up here. Sun jumpin like lightnin bugs off the water. A flash here, a flash there.

- *Wendy Jett*

Rocks so big I'm sure God can see em from heaven. The creek just seems to run on forever, right off the edge of the county.

I'm fallin. Fallin fast. My heart has pushed its way into my throat. Fallin toward Granny Faye's house. Fast, faster, faster, until I stop ... and float just outside the kitchen winda. Granny Faye's cookin. Looks like fried chicken and greens. I bet she has some of them big biscuits in the oven too. I hope she has enough for me to sit in. I tap on the winda. But she don't even know I'm here.

Then Granny drops her spoon. She starts to rub her arm. Then her head. What's wrong, Granny Faye? She sits in the chair. Grease poppin from the stove onto the counter. Granny Faye falls onto the floor. Grease poppin from the stove to the kitchen rug.

I need to tell Grandpap. But I can't fly no more, I can only float. Here, above Granny Faye. Smoke. Smoke from the rug. Grease a poppin.

Then Granny Faye sees me. She smiles. "I love you, girl."

I hear Grandpap's footsteps.

I am fallin, fallin backwards. Faster. I can't stop. Grandpap and Granny Faye are slippin far away. I am fallin.

Mama says, "Wake up girl, get up offa that couch. Sumthins happened to Granny Faye."

State Fair Apple

she presses blade
just under the skin
draws it toward her thumb

firm red hide pulled
gently from juicy yellow flesh

round and round
round and round

a perfect long spiral
of freckled fruit rind

drops
to the floor

- *Wendy Jett*

ReVisited

I love you girl. I'm sad to go.
I love you girl. I'll miss you so.

I love you girl. Take care of your mama.
I love you girl. I will see you one tomarra.

I love you granny. Please don't go.
I love you granny. I'll miss you so.

I love you granny. I know you can't stay.
I need you granny, with me every day.

I love you granny. I'll miss you so.
I love you granny. Please don't go.

I love you girl. I will see you one tomarra.
I love you girl. Take care of your mama.

I love you girl. I'll miss you so.
I love you girl. I'm sad to go.

Daddy

"Sona bitches! Bastards! Sona bitches!" I can hear Daddy hollerin. So I peep outta the door. Daddy throws his lunchbox cross the room and breaks Mama's picture on the wall. That picture belonged to Granny Faye's mama, Charlotte. There ain't no other picture like that in the county. Mama just watches Daddy. She don't say a word.

"They will burn in hell for what they did to us! 20 good men without a job. They will burn in hell." Daddy picks up the lunch box and throws it against the floor.

I can't see what Daddys' doin, but I think he's in the kitchen. Mama picks up the lunchbox but don't touch the broken picture. I hear the fridge open and the pop of a beer can.

Daddy's drinkin.

I close the bedroom door as quiet as I can. Petey's still sleepin. He needs to stay that way. I rub my finger cross that little dragonfly on his forehead, remindin God to keep Petey safe.

So now I sit here in front of the winda. Gazin at the glorious night sky. Watchin the trees sleep. Watchin the stars dance. Granny Faye said that nightime is when God nourishes our soul. He holds us safe in his arms and rocks away our worries. But he can only do that if you're sleepin. If you're awake, the worries of the earthly world creep their way into your heart. Worries about Daddy's job. Worries about Mama's picture. Worries about keepin

Petey safe. Worries about Grandpap feedin himself. The earthly world is fulla worries.

Mama says the easiest way to deal with earthly worries is to give em to God. She says if you just tell God your worries and ask him to carry them, he will. I think God might be tired of carryin my earthly worries. Seems like I've been givin him more and more of them lately. But I'm gonna try.

The best way to talk to God is on your knees. Mama says kneelin in the presence of God shows respect for the Lord Almighty. So I kneel, right in front of the winda. I ask God to carry Daddy's earthly worries. I ask God to carry Mama's earthly worries. I ask God to keep Petey and Grandpap safe and fed. I ask God to carry my earthly worries. At least for a little while.

I hear Petey rollin in the bed. Moanin and a groanin. He sits straight up like a beanpole and mumbles, "Sona bitches. Bastards."

Daddy's drinkin.

- *Wendy Jett*

Night

Light leaves the room
It's a dark, hollow tomb

Sona Bitch Daddys' Drinkin'

Just the pop of a can
Inside a strong hand

Sona Bitch Daddys' Drinkin'

Sleep will not come
For daughter or son

SonaBitch Daddys' Drinkin'

The nights are so long
When Daddys' so wrong

Sona Bitch Daddys' Drinkin

Daddy's Day After Drinkin Breakfast

½ of a beer (save the other ½ for lunch)
2 big spoons of Granny's Hot Sauce
Tomato juice
2 raw eggs-scrambled

Put the beer in a tall glass
Add the Hot Sauce and eggs
Fill the rest of the glass with Tomato Juice
Drink it all down without takin a breath

Talkin

In all the years of my life, I ain't never seen her smoke a cigarette. Never. But there she sits, at the kitchen table, with one of Daddy's cigarettes in her mouth. Eyes closed. Coffee steamin from the cup. Hands a folded in her lap. If you can pray with a cigarette in your mouth, I think that's what she's doin. Prayin.

Mama says it ain't proper to interrupt a conversation with God, so I just sit and wait. Bout that time she opens her eyes and sees me.

"What you doin outta bed girl? You know tomorra's a school day." Mamma puts the cigarette in her coffee. I hear it sizzle before it goes belly up in the cup.

Mamma turns her chair toward me and motions for me to sit. I love to sit on Mama's lap. Some might say I'm too big for it, but Mama says there ain't no such thing. She says there's always enough room on a Mama's lap for her babies.

I climb up and she pushes my hair back behind my ear. "We need to do somethin bout that hair, girl. You look like you been livin in the barn." She kisses my forehead. I lay my head on her chest just so I can hear her heartbeat. It's a beatin fast. Sounds like one of them drums in the marchin band. Rat a tat a tat a tat. Boom, boom, boom.

"What's wrong, Mama? Your hearts a beatin so fast."

- *Wendy Jett*

"Sometimes the heart tries to run away from earthly worries. Sometimes it runs fast. Tonight's one of those nights, girl. Don't you fret over it. I gave my worries to God, he will carry them til tomorra."

Mama starts to hum. I'm sure it's a hymn but I don't know which one. She takes her finger and traces the scar on my knee. It's shaped just like a crescent moon. I slipped on a rock in the creek and sliced that knee open. Mama taped it up, good and clean, but it never healed proper. Daddy said I wouldn't sit still long enough for it to heal right. I guess that's true.

"How's that tooth comin along?" Mama gives me a wink.

"Don't be pullin my tooth, Mama. It's not nearly loose enough." I give it a wiggle just so she can see the time ain't right. "Where's Daddy?"

Mama shifts in the chair and pulls me a little closer. "He's out walkin. He'll be home soon." She starts to rock side to side, hummin a little louder.

"Why's Daddy out walkin in the night, Mama?" I tilt my head up and see that her eyes are closed.

"I hope he's talkin with God, girl. Sometimes a man has to get out in the darkness of the night to see the light of day."

I hear the pit-pat of feet on the kitchen floor. Sure enough. Petey's up. Mama turns and motions for him to sit. I scooch over so he can sit on one leg while I take the other. Petey's feet are cold, he musta been sleepin with them stickin outta the blanket again. Mama takes her finger and traces the dragonfly on Petey's forehead. He closes his eyes and pushes his head against Mama's chest. I'm sure he's listenin to that marchin band.

"How's that tooth comin along?" Mamma gives me a wink. She pushes my hair back behind my ear. "We gotta do somethin about that hair, girl. You look like you been livin in the barn."

• *Wendy Jett*

Listenin

Listen closely
little girl,
to the space between
the words. It has a voice
of its own, like a candle
it slowly burns.

Sometimes it's not
what we say, but
what lingers there within.
Hidin' between
the breaths we take,
the true meaning does begin.

Daughter

I pluck my eyes out
place them in
a little white box
with a big pink ribbon.

Give it to her.

I want her to see
what I see
the next time she
looks in the mirror.

Daisy

Daddy said he shot her. Said she deserved it. Daddy said, "Any dog that bites the hand that feeds it, is a beast. And beasts need to be sent straight back to hell." Daisy don't have a mean bone in her body. I know she was just protectin her babies. That's what mamas are supposed to do. Protect their babies. She probly thought Daddy was gonna take them babies and toss em in the creek like he did with the kittens last spring. Mamas know things daddies can never know.

Mamas know how to grow babies in their bodies. How to use the milk in their titties to feed them babies. Daddies don't know nothin bout that. Daddies only know how to chop wood and drink beer and shoot good dogs.

Now that Daisy's gone, I'm sure he's takin them babies down to the woods. I'm gonna find em and hide em in the shed. I'm gonna be a good mama to them babies so they can grow up to be good dogs like Daisy.

I gotta be careful Daddy don't see me. Mama says he's a good man with just a teaspoon of meanness. But I don't want no part of that teaspoon.

I love walkin in the woods. God's country. If you listen close enough, you can hear angels singin in the woods. Songs about the glory of God's creation. The birds and crickets sing along. The wind whispers with them angels. The power of God is strong in the woods.

- *Wendy Jett*

The world was born in the woods. The Garden of Eden. God planted his garden millions of years ago. Planted flowers, trees, corn, maters. He put good dogs in that garden. God loves dogs. Dogs like Daisy. I'm sure Daisy is tucked up under God's feet right now, as he sits on the throne of righteousness.

Well, there's that sack. Layin on the bank. Looks like Daddy didn't take the time to drown them babies. One, two, three, four, but all are dead. Dead like Daisy. Gone to heaven to be with their mama.

Mamas and babies are supposed to be together. They need each other. It don't matter how old you are, you are always your mama's baby. Babies carry pieces of their mama's soul inside them. When mamas leave this earth, that piece of soul is ripped right outta that baby. Some babies are never the same after their mama goes to heaven. They always feel like a piece is missin.

Mama says that's what we call grief. She says grief about killed her when Granny Faye passed. Mama says grief is the cost of love, but it's worth it. She says mamas want their babies to make it through the grief and live a good life. I guess Daisy's babies didn't know that. They let grief smother their little souls, their little bodies. I'm gonna give them babies a good, Christian burial. They deserve it. They was good dogs, just like their mama, Daisy.

Jump Rope

Daisy Dog, Daisy Dog, turn around
Daisy Dog, Daisy Dog buried in the ground.

Daisy Dog, Daisy Dog love you so,
Daisy Dog, Daisy Dog sad to see you go.

How many tears did I cry?
One, two, three, four, five, six, seven, eight….

- *Wendy Jett*

If You're Mad at Your Daddy Clap Your Hands

If you're mad at your daddy clap your hands
If you're mad at your daddy clap your hands
If you're mad at your daddy
And you think he's really nasty
If you're mad at your daddy clap your hands

If you wish he wasn't your daddy stomp your feet
If you wish he wasn't your daddy stomp your feet
Cause if he wasn't your daddy
You know you'd be so happy
If you wish he wasn't your daddy stomp your feet

If you want Daisy not your daddy say Hurrah!
If you want Daisy not your daddy say Hurrah!
Cause Daisy was a good dog
And Daddy's just a tailed frog
If you want Daisy not your daddy say Hurrah!

Mama Says

Mama says Satan plants seeds. Mama says them seeds can take root even in the heart of a good man. She says all we can do is pray that the roots don't settle in. Shallow roots, that's what we want. Shallow roots wither in the presence of God.

I've seen Satan plant his seeds. I've seen them seeds take root. Take root in a good man's heart. My daddy's heart.

I've watched God's presence grab hold of them roots and pull them, like weeds, out of a good man's heart. My daddy's heart.

But this time is different. Them roots are settlin in. Weavin their way through my daddy's veins. Through my daddy's muscles. Through my daddy's bones. I think them roots have snaked their way into my daddy's soul.

Daddy pushed Petey's face right into his mashed taters tonight. Petey hates mashed taters, but Daddy said, "That's no excuse not to eat what Mama fixed."

Mama wiped Petey's face and told Daddy, "Now that's no way to treat one of our babies."

Daddy told Mama to "shut up."

Them seeds have taken root. Them roots are settlin in. Them roots are goin deep.

Mama said, "Go on, girl, put Petey to bed for me. I'll finish these dishes."

Daddy said, "Bring me another beer, girl."

I let Petey wear his favorite jammies. Anybody that has their face pushed into their mashed taters should get to wear their favorite jammies. We prayed together. We prayed that them roots don't run deep. We prayed for shallow roots.

But I hear them roots growin. I hear em goin deep. Them roots are takin over a good man's heart.

Them roots smell like beer and cigarettes. Them roots sound like the smack of a hand against a good woman's face. The crash of a lamp to the floor. Them roots are settlin in.

Mama says God is forgivin. She says we can walk in the footsteps of God and forgive. Mama says the power of love is strong. She says the roots of love run deep. Deeper than any root from the seed of Satan. But I think Mama's wrong. Satan's roots settle in. Take hold. Satan's roots run very deep.

Tonight them roots are thick in my daddy's heart. Satan is sowin seeds, seeds are takin root quicker than God can forgive.

The thump of a good woman's head against the wall. Not once, not twice, but three times. Them roots hollerin at Petey to quit cryin.

Satan can sow seeds in a good girl's heart. Them seeds can take root. Them roots can settle in, run deep. Deep into the veins, the muscles, the bones of a good girl. Settle into the soul of a good girl. Them roots know just where Daddy keeps his gun.

Mama says courage is doin what has to be done even though we're scared. She says courage don't have to grow roots. It can stand on its own. Mama says, "Be courageous girl."

Boy

Snips and snails
and puppy dog tails
are what little boys should know.

Not

Smacks and slaps
and long boot straps
for they are a heavy load.

- *Wendy Jett*

Girl

Satan is strong, but
God is forgivin.
Sometimes it's so
hard to just
keep on livin.

In a world fulla
meaness, a girl stands
alone, to face
her worst fears, inside
her own home.

Fate

- *Wendy Jett*

He's buried next to the big Oak with them boy babies. Mama said that was the best place for him to spend eternity. I guess them boy babies probly keep him company so he don't feel alone.

Mama says busted teeth and broken arms can heal pretty fast, but a broken soul takes much longer. She says it takes lots of prayer and walkin in the woods. I know my arm will mend, but I don't think my soul will. It's always gonna have a hole in it the shape of a dragonfly. Petey was special. He was a special gift from God. I guess God missed him and needed him to come back home.

Daddy ain't said one word since that night. He never told Mama he was sorry. He never told me he was sorry. I bet he never even told God he was sorry. I'm hopin he swallowed his forked tongue and never talks again. Mama says Daddy's broken. I think Daddy's been broke my whole life. He ain't never gonna be fixed. God will hang a millstone round his neck and make him carry it the rest of his life for what he's done.

Mama says hate will eat you up from the inside out. I feel like somethin ate me and spit me back out. I am filled with spite. I know I need to find it in my heart to forgive Daddy, but my heart ain't big enough for that. A broken heart can't forgive.

Grandpap howled like a wolf when Mama told him what happened to Petey. I never heard a man make them noises before. Never saw a grown man cry all his tears out, but that's what Grandpap did. He cried til his eyes dried up and bled. He ain't got outta bed since then.

Mama's skinny as a corn stalk. Says she ain't hungry. She's been smokin cigarettes and drinkin coffee all night long since we buried Petey. I see her out there talkin to Petey in the moonlight. Some nights she lays on top him so he remembers her. I told her Petey will always remember his mama cause she is a good woman. I guess she don't believe me.

I asked Billy Wade to paint Mama a picture of Petey, but he said he can't lift his body to paint. Said the weight of Petey's passin is too heavy.

Pastor John said a nice prayer for Petey in church Sunday. He said God wraps his arms round children when they get to heaven. He kisses them and sings them a lullaby every night fore they climb into their beds. I hope God remembers to cover Petey's feet good and tight. He always wriggles outta them covers.

I'm gonna take me a walk in the woods. Listen to them angels singin with the wind. Maybe I will lay myself down in that butterfly field and talk to Petey. I'm sure he's with Granny Faye and Daisy. I won't never be with them again, seein that I won't be goin to heaven. Satan has planted his spiteful seed in my heart and God won't have no part of that. I am broken, just like my daddy.

- *Wendy Jett*

Dragonfly Lullaby Reprise

Petey boy spread them wings,
Fly to heaven where you can sing.

Granny Faye will hold you tight,
Go on boy take now your flight.

Dragonfly, dragonfly, Angels sing,
Angels a sittin on a dragonfly wing.
Dragonfly, dragonfly, Angels sing,
Angels a sittin on a dragonfly wing.

Over the moon chase them stars,
To heaven's gate it ain't far.

Oh, sweet one we love you boy,
You were a dragonfly that brought us joy.

Dragonfly, dragonfly, Angels sing,
Angels a sittin on a dragonfly wing.
Dragonfly, dragonfly, Angels sing,
Petey a sittin on a dragonfly wing.

Little Boy Blue Reprise

Forgive your daddy
Little Boy Blue
My heart is broken
For what I done to you

You were my blessing
That was ripped away
By a vengeful God
To make me pay

For mistakes I made
Throughout my life
For the pain I caused
My children and wife

Faith

Girl •

It's been near a year since Petey passed. Grandpap passed few months after. Mama said he died of grief. I'm sure Granny Faye and Petey was happy to see him at heaven's gate. They probly had a big ol supper to celebrate. I bet Granny even baked a pie.

Mama seems to be doin better since she started workin at Johnson's store. She works the cash register, and they let her sell her baskets there too. Haven't seen her smoke a cigarette in a few weeks. We ain't seen Daddy in a long time. Mama says he's just livin in the hills. That's ok with me. I don't want him round here nohow.

Guess I need to work on my forgiveness. I been tryin. Been readin Proverbs. Learnin bout King Solomon. Pastor John says the King was a wise man. That I can learn a lot about speakin gently and kindly bout people, even my daddy. Pastor says that God blesses those who learn to hold their tongues and follow wise advice. He says just cause you forgive someone, it don't mean you like what they did.

Mama got me a dog. Said it might help take the edge offa being without Petey. I named him Huckleberry. He's a good dog. He loves walkin in the woods with me. We been crossin the creek, and walkin up to McClure's farm. They got the prettiest pine forest you ever seen. The trees are so thick it looks like nighttime when you get up under em. Smells good too. Like Christmas. Sometimes me and Huckleberry just lay up under there and sing. Hymns mostly.

Just yesterday we was comin back cross the creek and Huckleberry just started a barkin. He was standin right in the middle of the creek. I got to lookin closer, and I saw what he was a barkin at. There musta been 100 dragonflies on one of them big rocks. They was all just sunnin themselves. Then one of them dragonflies landed right on my shoulder. Just sat there, lookin at me. I tried to see the angel sittin on the wing, but the sun was too bright. I told that angel to tell Petey we miss him but we're doin ok. It just flew off cross the bank.

I told Mama what happened. She said she was sure my message would get to Petey. She told me all we can do is have faith that the angel made it back to heaven safe. Faith is somethin you carry in your heart, right next to love and family. Mama says the faith of a comin rainbow is what gets us through the storm. She says the faith of a new day is what wakes us up every mornin with the sun. I think Mama's right.

- *Wendy Jett*

Acknowledgments

Many thanks to The Carnegie Center for Literacy and Learning in Lexington, Kentucky, particularly Marcia Thornton Jones, Neil Chethik and Lynn Pruett, for their support and encouragement.

There are no words to express the gratitude I have for Katerina Stoykova. A wonderful teacher, mentor, poet and human being. Thank you for all you do for the writing community and for all the wisdom you have shared with me.

Lastly, a big thanks to my dad, Bud, for all the hours he shared stories of his childhood, friends, family and this amazing place we call home.

About the Author

Wendy Jett is a long time fitness instructor, decoupage nerd, Improv junkie and loves to write. She is a born and raised Kentucky girl and now calls Lexington home. Mom to two humans, Kayla and Stevie and one canine, Lola Jolene, she does the best she can every day! Some days she does better than others.